My First NFL Book

BUFFALO BILLS

Nate Cohn

Go to **www.av2books.com**, and enter this book's unique code.

BOOK CODE

P425579

AV² by Weigl brings you media enhanced books that support active learning.

AV² provides enriched content that supplements and complements this book. Weigl's AV² books strive to create inspired learning and engage young minds in a total learning experience.

Your AV² Media Enhanced books come alive with...

Audio
Listen to sections of the book read aloud.

Video
Watch informative video clips.

Embedded Weblinks
Gain additional information for research.

Try This!
Complete activities and hands on experiments.

Key Words
Study vocabulary, and complete a matching word activity.

Quizzes
Test your knowledge.

Slide Show
View images and captions, and prepare a presentation.

... and much, much more!

Published by AV² by Weigl
350 5th Avenue, 59th Floor
New York, NY 10118

Website: www.av2books.com

Copyright ©2018 AV² by Weigl

Library of Congress Control Number: 2017930536

ISBN 978-1-4896-5484-7 (hardcover)
ISBN 978-1-4896-5486-1 (multi-user eBook)

Printed in the United States of America in Brainerd, Minnesota
1 2 3 4 5 6 7 8 9 0 21 20 19 18 17

032017
020317

Editor: Katie Gillespie
Art Director: Terry Paulhus

Weigl acknowledges Getty Images, Newscom, and iStock as the primary image suppliers for this title.

My First NFL Book

BUFFALO BILLS

CONTENTS

Team History

The Buffalo Bills began playing football in 1960. Ralph Wilson started both the team and the league they first played in. The Bills joined the NFL in 1970. They are the only NFL team with a stadium in the state of New York.

The team is named for cowboy "Buffalo Bill" Cody. He did rope tricks in traveling shows.

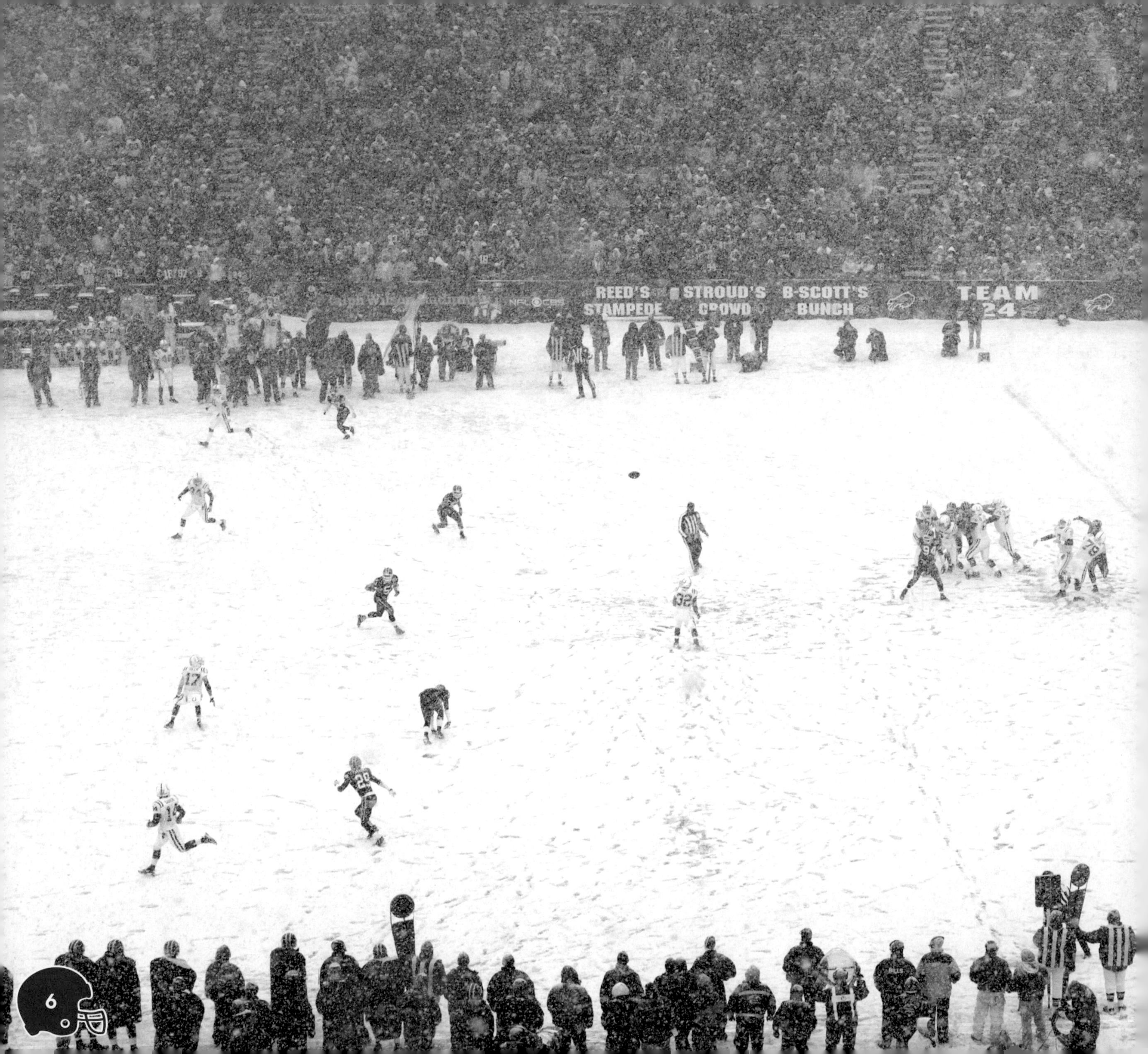
REED'S STAMPEDE
STROUD'S CROWD
B-SCOTT'S BUNCH
TEAM 24

The Stadium

The Bills' stadium is called New Era Field. It is near Lake Erie. This is a part of the country that can get very cold. Snow forms over the lake and falls on the field. The Bills sometimes offer free tickets to fans if they help shovel snow away.

New Era Field is in Orchard Park, New York. It is near the city of Buffalo.

Team Spirit

Billy Buffalo is the mascot who cheers on the team. He looks like the American bison that used to roam the New York area. The main difference is that Billy has bright blue hair. He joined the team in 2000.

Billy Buffalo has his initials on his jersey instead of a number.

8

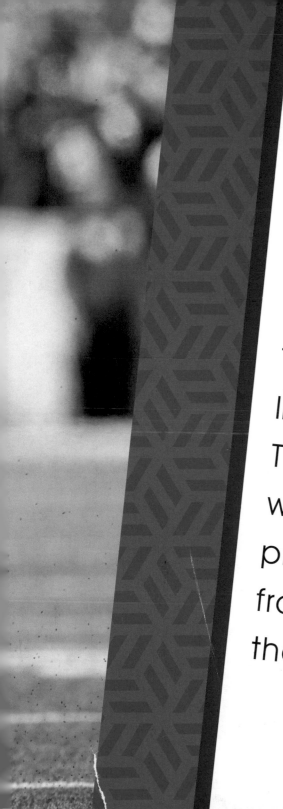

The Jerseys

The Bills' first uniforms were blue, white, and silver. These colors were changed in 1962. Their jerseys looked too much like another team's jerseys. The Bills' colors became blue, white, and red instead. New players pick their numbers from a special list of numbers that former players wore.

The Helmet

The Bills' first logo was a red bison standing still. This was changed to a blue bison in 1974. The animal looks like it is charging forward. It has a big red streak to make it look fast. The Bills' helmets have the logo on each side.

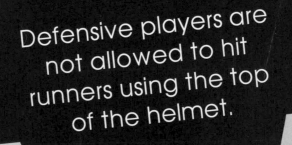

Defensive players are not allowed to hit runners using the top of the helmet.

13

The Coach

The Bills' head coach is Sean McDermott. He was hired at the end of the 2016 season. He coached many NFL defensive teams before joining the Bills. The players he used to coach were in the top 10 of NFL defenses. The last team he coached went to the Super Bowl.

Player Positions

The offense has four chances to move the ball 10 yards. A punter is often called in when this does not happen in three tries. This player kicks the ball down the field so the other team has a hard time scoring during their turn.

Most NFL players still playing at age 40 or older are punters or kickers.

Sammy Watkins is a wide receiver for the Bills. He was drafted in 2014. Watkins is one of the fastest players in the NFL. He is also known for making hard catches. Watkins had five games with at least 100 receiving yards in 2015. He had 822 receiving yards in his first 13 games. This set a team record.

Bruce Smith was a Bills defensive end. He holds the NFL record for most sacks. A sack is when a player tackles a quarterback before the ball can be thrown. Smith made 200 sacks over his career. He made 171 of these sacks with the Bills. He joined the Pro Football Hall of Fame in 2009.

Team Records

The Bills are the only team to play four Super Bowls in a row. This happened in the early 1990s. Their quarterback then was Jim Kelly. He is also known for scoring 237 career touchdowns. Steve Christie kicked a 54-yard field goal in the Super Bowl for the 1993 season. It is the longest field goal in Super Bowl history.

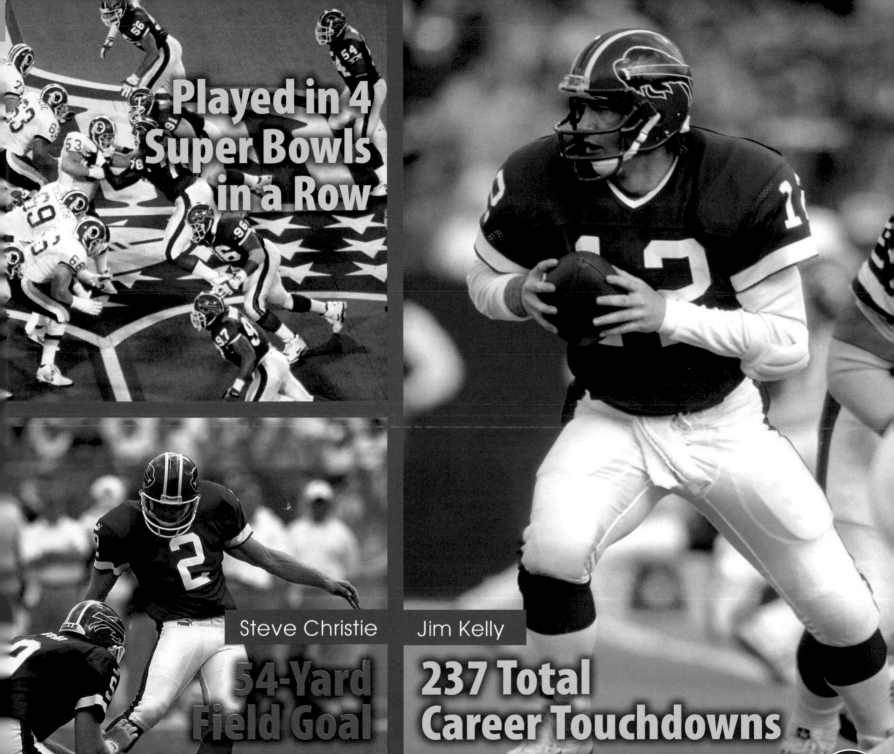

Played in 4
Super Bowls
in a Row

Steve Christie   Jim Kelly

54-Yard
Field Goal

237 Total
Career Touchdowns

21

By the Numbers

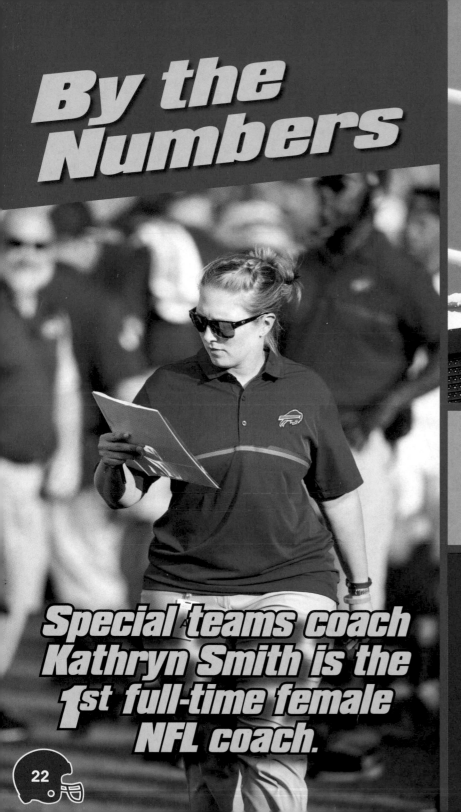

Special teams coach Kathryn Smith is the 1st full-time female NFL coach.

New Era Field can seat **73,079** fans.

The Bills have changed owners just 1 time in their history.

Bills fans once removed **220,000 tons** of snow from the field.

The Bills won a 1993 game after being **32 points** behind in the third quarter.

Running back Thurman Thomas set a team record by rushing for **11,938 yards.**

Quiz

1. Who started the Buffalo Bills?

2. In what year did Billy Buffalo join the team?

3. Who is the Bills' head coach?

4. How many Super Bowls did the Bills play in a row in the 1990s?

5. Who kicked the longest field goal in Super Bowl history?

ANSWERS 1. Ralph Wilson 2. 2000 3. Sean McDermott 4. Four 5. Steve Christie

24